Thy Word Is Forever Established in Heaven

Thy Word Is Forever Established in Heaven

Put Your Voice to God's Word!
A Daily Devotional

Toni Allen

Strategic Book Publishing
www.sbpra.net

For information about special discounts for bulk purchases, please contact Strategic Book Publishing, Special Sales, at bookorder@sbpra.net.

ISBN: 978-1-68235-755-2

DEDICATION

I give honor and glory to my awesome and wonderful Lord and Savior, Jesus Christ, who has strengthened and empowered me to continue to proclaim His Gospel and goodness through writing.

This book was inspired by the Holy Spirit and is dedicated to every believer in Jesus and those coming into the faith. God wants us to understand the importance of His Word and, when used properly, how it can and will transform our lives and environment. The Word of God is Spirit and Life and it releases life wherever we send it. Friends, let's begin to put our voice to the Word of God and be a witness to **Isaiah 55:11**:

> So shall my word be that goeth forth out of my mouth; it shall not return unto me void; but it shall accomplish that which I please and it shall prosper in the thing where to I sent it.

ACKNOWLEDGEMENTS

As always, I want to thank Lynn and the team at Strategic Book Publishing, for the confidence and professionalism that were placed on this project. I pray that God continues to bless you and your team beyond your expectations.

Friends and family: Thanks to all who supported and encouraged me through this journey. Thank you for every encouraging word, every prayer, and every seed that was sown into my life to keep me moving forward. I pray that God will continue to bless you beyond measures and grant you your heart's desire as you grow in Him.

INTRODUCTION

Psalms 119:89: "Forever Lord, Your Word is settled in Heaven."

The eternal Word of God is firmly forever settled and established in Heaven. God wants us to understand the power and authority of His Word. As believers in Christ, we must identify with and understand that we are God's legal authority on Earth. Therefore, we have the awesome responsibility and duty to speak God's Word and bring some of Heaven's goodness into history (Earth).

Notice that the above scripture doesn't say that your "Word" is forever settled in "Heaven" and "Earth." Why? In order for God's Word to be established on Earth, it needs a human voice to activate and release it into the earth. It all started in the Garden of Eden, when the Lord God created man and gave him dominion over the earth. God blessed them and said unto them "be fruitful, multiply, replenish, subdue the earth and have dominion over every living thing that moveth upon the earth" (**Genesis 1:28**). However, we see in scriptures (**Genesis 3:1-6**) that Satan entered and convinced them to disobey God. With this disobedience they relinquished their authority to Satan, and no longer had the power and authority to subdue the earth. Our amazing, omniscient God had a plan, and that plan was to wrap Himself in flesh, temporarily leave His Glorious residence, and become a part of His creation to reconnect mankind back to Him and restore the authority to rule Earth as He intended and designed. This is all possible because of Jesus's completed work on Calvary. Although God's Word can work apart from mankind's intervention, He gave us the opportunity to partner with Him to rule and advance His Kingdom on Earth.

We, as believers in Christ, have been empowered by the Holy Spirit, to be God's legal representatives on Earth. We have the divine ability and power to shape and reshape our environment, our surroundings, ministries, homes, and lives to align with the Word of God by speaking His Word and praying His Word. That is why it is imperative that we learn and understand God's Word, so we can speak God's language (Kingdom language) into our history.

The Word of God is inerrant, flawless, faultless, and pure. In short it is PERFECT and it will transform you, others, and your environment if handled properly. Not only should we continually speak the word of God, we should make it a habit to pray the Word of God. When you don't know where to start praying, or can't think of anything to pray about, open your bible and begin to pray through the scriptures. This book is designed to heighten our awareness of the power of God's Word and incorporate His Word in our prayers. In essence, we are putting our voice to the Word! When we put our voice to the Word, we will begin to witness shifts and changes in our situations and environments because we are speaking Kingdom language and our God watches over His Word to perform it. **Jeremiah 1:12** affirms that: "Then said the Lord unto me, thou has well seen, I will hasten my Word to perform it." The word "hasten" means to be quick to do something (Oxford Dictionary). I am sure all of us want to see God quickly change or intervene in a bad situation or circumstance.

If we are going to maintain our victory on Earth and witness the supernatural move of God, we must remember that the battle is won on our knees in prayer. We are in a spiritual battle; therefore, it must be fought with the mighty spiritual weapons provided by God, which is prayer and His Word. These are not the only spiritual weapons, but these are the two that we are focusing on in this book. Always remember the Word (the Holy Scriptures) is God and He is the only one who has and will continue to destroy Satan and the power of darkness. When we pray the Word, we are releasing the power of God into our situation and into the spiritual realm. This is how we uproot, tear down, and destroy strongholds that keep us in bondage. And **Hebrews 4:12** tells us that: "The Word of God is quick and powerful and sharper than any two-edged sword."

Wow, I do not know about you, friend, but knowing that I can cut, slice, and block the works of the devil occurring in my life and in my loved one's lives, cities, neighborhoods, nations, etc., I am encouraged to learn God's Word, so that I can pray and witness transformation.

This devotional book is designed as a book of prayers, with thirty-two scriptures, life applications, sample prayers around the scripture, and a space for you to develop a prayer and take notes. These compilations of scriptures are intended to deliberately and intentionally guide you in using God's Word in your prayers. The intent is to daily pray, mediate, and study a scripture so that it can become a part of your daily life. If you are serious about elevating your prayer life, begin praying God's Word and watch God come for His Word as He did with the Prophet Daniel. The word is declared in **Daniel 10:12**:

> Then said he unto me, Fear not, Daniel; for from the first day that thou didst set thine heart to understand, and to chasten thyself before thy God, thy words were heard and I am come for thy words.

When we pray God's will and purpose, He will come for His Word to perform it.

It is with great astonishment to know that God hears us, but to know and hear Him say, " I have come for your words" is amazement on a higher level. To know this inspires me to dive deep into God's Word, to arm myself in prayer for spiritual warfare! Are you ready to put your voice to the Word of God!

God has placed within my spirit to always inform readers. In order to activate and release God's Word in our lives, (1) we must be born again of the spirit of God and (2) we must be in right standing with God. The Word of God works, and God doesn't want His people losing faith in His Word or being destroyed by Satan, because we are out of His safety net. The Word of God is not empty promises or false hope. We must learn how to position and posture our hearts to receive, activate, and release His Word into the situations, circumstances, etc. If you have not accepted Jesus Christ as your Lord and Savior, you may fast forward to the end of the book and recite the "Repentance" Prayer. If you have accepted Jesus as your Lord and Savior, but may not be in right standing with the Lord. His word tells us in **1 John 1:9**: "If we confess our sins, He is faithful and just to forgive us our sins, and to cleanse us from all unrighteousness!"

(Unless otherwise noted, all scriptures are from the King James version of the bible.)

Now we are ready to be God's mouthpiece on earth!

DAY ONE

Isaiah 41:10: "Fear thou not; for I am with thee: be not dismayed; for I am thy God: I will strengthen thee; yea, I will help thee; yea I will uphold thee with the right hand of my righteousness."

Life Application:

What are you facing today that you need to be reminded that you are being kept with God's victorious right hand of power? And, remember, who sits at the right of God? Exactly, our Righteous Lord and Savior, Jesus Christ. Friend, lean back in Jesus's strong arms and know that He knows how to strengthen and sustain you when a life crisis appears to overwhelm you. So, fear not and rest in His strength and power. There is no problem too big or too small for our God. All power and all authority have been given to the Son, in Heaven, Earth, and beneath the earth.

Prayer:

Father, thank you for strengthening and holding me up with your victorious right hand of righteousness and power. Because of Your victorious hand, I have nothing to fear and can face today and every day with confidence knowing You are with me (If you have a specific situation, name it here). In Jesus's name, Amen.

Your prayer for today:

Notes:

DAY TWO

Isaiah 43:2: "When thou passest through the waters, I will be with thee; and through the rivers, they shall not overflow thee: when thou walkest through the fire, thou shall not be burned; neither shall the flame kindle upon thee."

Life Application:

You may be going through a difficult time right now. It may seem like there is no light at the end. It looks as though the fire of life is going to overtake you. You are drowning in bills, the children have gotten on your last nerve, you lost your job, your husband or wife does not understand you, and everywhere you turn there is a problem and no solution! Your mother, father, and friends do not have time for you, because they have their own situations. In other words, you are drowning in this journey called "life." Who can you turn to? If this is your story today, know that Jesus is always available and ready to listen and provide help. Don't give in, don't give up, and don't lose hope. His word affirms that He is with you!

Prayer:

Lord, I give You praise for making yourself real to me. Even though I'm going through this situation, I know You are with me. You said when I pass through the waters, You will be with me, they shall not overflow me, and the fire of life shall not burn or kindle upon me. I shall be like the children of Israel and walk through this situation as on dry land to my victory. In Jesus's precious name, Amen.

Your prayer for today:

____

____

____

____

____

Notes:

DAY THREE

Psalm 91:15: "He shall call upon me, and I will answer him, I will be with him in trouble; I will deliver him and honor him."

Life Application:

I love the honesty and pureness of God! This scripture lets us know that we are going to have times of trouble. Everything, every day, is not going to be a bed of roses (that's Heaven) in this lifetime. However, we are assured that when we call upon the name of the Lord, and His name is Jesus, He will answer and deliver us. His timing, His method of deliverance, may not always be what **we** expect or what **we** want, or He may not even deliver us from the specific circumstance, but know that God's timing and way is always perfect for us. He is our ultimate Protection from danger. I place special emphasis on the fact that we must know His name (Jesus) and continually abide in His truth if we expect an answer and deliverance. When we meet this condition, then we may stand barefoot, shoulders squared back, head and chin lifted in confidence, and expect that the Lord, my God, will deliver and honor me when I call upon His name ... Jesus!

Prayer:

Glory to the One and only True and Living God. Lord, You are faithful, and because of Your faithfulness and my covenant relationship with You, I can rejoice in this trial, adversity, and or struggle that I'm facing today. Lord, You promised that when I call upon Your name, You will answer, deliver, and honor me. Today, I'm calling upon the mighty, strong, powerful name of Jesus; that name is my strong tower, one I can run to for security. Lord, if You choose not to deliver me, I know that You are with me and I am honored with your goodness, grace, and love. I seal this prayer in Jesus's name ... Amen.

Your prayer for today:

Notes:

DAY FOUR

Psalm 92:12: "The righteous shall flourish like the palm tree; he shall grow like a cedar in Lebanon."

Life Application:

This promise is loaded with power. God wants us to acquire a deeper understanding of His Word, so we can activate and release that power. The body of Christ is God's legal representative on Earth and we have the power within our mouths to establish standards, shift the atmosphere, and make a difference wherever we go! It's not by accident or a coincidence that the "righteous" in the bible are characterized by "palm trees." Palm trees symbolize strength, sturdiness, vitality, and long life. Wow, this is how God sees His people! Cedars in Lebanon represent strength, elevation, immortality, resilience, and power. To sum up these characteristics, our destiny as believers is to be powerful, plenteous, strong, unmovable, and to enjoy a long fruitful life. This promise excites and encourages me to want to dive deeper into God's Word, so I can get a clearer view of who I am in Him. I pray that you are excited and encouraged as well!

Prayer:

Father, thank you for all your promises and blessings. Lord, Your word attest that the righteous shall be planted and flourish like the palm trees. Thank you, Lord, that when You see me You see the righteousness of your Son, Jesus. It is because of His righteousness in me that I can boldly stand before you and proclaim that I am righteous, I shall flourish, I am powerful, I am unmovable, and I shall enjoy a long productive life in You. Thank you, Lord, that goodness and mercy shall be my portion in life. In Jesus's name, Amen!

Your prayer for today:

____

____

____

____

____

Notes:

DAY FIVE

2 Chronicles 16:9: "For the eyes of the Lord run to and fro throughout the whole earth, to shew Himself strong in the behalf of them whose heart is perfect toward Him."

Life Application:

Our awesome God is omnipresent, omnipotent, and omniscient. Nothing is hidden from Him. He sees and knows everything. God's eyes are always watching for that faithful, hungry servant that He can prove His faithfulness to. Wow, how amazing, our God wants to prove Himself to His humanity. God is looking for **faith**; He is not looking for our self-righteousness. Imagine, when God looks down upon you, upon me, and sees our faith, His eyes lock in on us! Our faith causes Him to incline upon His throne and gaze upon us. His eyes latch upon our faith, and we have captured His attention!

Now, he is ready to show Himself strong on our behalf. Whatever problem or situation you are facing, let your faith draw God towards you, so He can show you His power and strength.

Prayer:

Blessed be the God that created the heavens and the earth! You are mighty and strong. I echo the psalmist when he states,

"Where can I go from your presence?" Lord, You are everywhere. There is nowhere I can go to hide from Your glorious presence. You see all and You know all. That's the beauty of serving an Omniscient, Omnipotent, and Omnipresent God; there is none like You. Lord, as your eyes roam throughout the earth, let my faith capture Your gaze. As Your Word declares that You are seeking someone to show your strength. Lord, here I am. I'm answering the call. Show Yourself strong in my situation—my family, my ministry, my marriage, in school—so that those around me will see your great power and know that there is a God that rules and reigns in Heaven and Earth! In Jesus's Holy name, Amen.

Your prayer for today:

____

____

____

____

____

Notes:

DAY SIX

Romans 8:37-39: "Nay, in all these things we are more than conquerors through Him that loved us. (38) For I am persuaded, that neither death, nor life, nor angels, nor principalities, nor powers, nor things present, nor things to come, (39) nor height, nor depth, nor any other creature, shall be able to separate us from the love of God, which is in Christ Jesus our Lord."

Life Application:

Friend, I don't know about you, but this is a promise for backflips! In this life we are going to be confronted with hardships. However, our God has assured us, that it doesn't matter what life brings to us, we are not **just** conquerors, but we are **more than** conquerors. A conqueror takes complete control over a place by military power and strength. God states that we are more than conquerors, more than victors. In short, we are invincible in **Christ!** It is because of Christ's victory at the Cross, burial, resurrection, ascension, and seating that we can boldly profess and stand on this promise. God's love for His people is intense and nothing can change that or separate us from His love. This should make us feel undefeatable. We can overwhelmingly overcome every adverse situation!

Prayer:

Father, thank you for Your unfailing love towards me. It is Your love that sustains me, upholds me, and places my feet on the solid rock, which is Jesus. It was Your great love for me that propelled Jesus to complete the task of the cross. It was love that held Him to the cross, and He saw me on the other side of that old rugged cross. And, because of this love, I can and will confront and overcome this situation (You can be specific). For I am more than a conqueror, I am undefeated in Christ and today I securely stand in Your love. In Jesus's name, Amen.

Your prayer for today:

____

____

____

____

____

Notes:

DAY SEVEN

Proverbs 3:5-6: "Trust in the Lord with all thy heart; and lean not unto thine own understanding. (v6) In all thy ways acknowledge Him, and He shall direct thy paths."

Life Application:

What an awesome feeling it is to serve a God who cares so much about us, wants to be involved in every detail of our lives, and is willing to take time to lead us. God is mindful of us and the path that we take in life. He does not want us to go down the wrong path (but if we do, He will redirect our steps when we acknowledge Him). He is so gentle that He will not force His ways upon us. He desires us to willingly acknowledge and invite Him to lead and guide us by His Spirit. God is always willing to guide us, instruct us, and lead us, but we must surrender our ways unto Him. We must invite Him in and allow Him to feel comfortable in every area of our lives. Because of His omniscient, omnipotent, and omnipresence prowess, He knows what our tomorrow looks like and what is best for us. Therefore, we can trust His way and His will for our lives. We do not necessarily have to understand his way or will, because we know His character. He is a good and faithful God and everything that He wants for us is good, acceptable, and perfect.

Prayer:

Heavenly Father, You know all and see all. You know my beginning from my ending; therefore, I confidently place my life and this (situation) in Your hands and I trust that You will give me clarity and directions. You said if I trust You and acknowledge You in all my ways, You will direct my path. Lord, thank you for making my path clear. In Jesus's name, Amen!

Your prayer for today:

____

____

____

____

____

Notes:

DAY EIGHT

Psalm 32:8: "I will instruct thee and teach thee in the way which thou shalt go; I will guide thee with mine eye."

Life Application:

This is a comforting promise. With so much distraction, confusion, chaos, and so many decisions we have to make on a daily basis, life can become quite overwhelming. It is sometimes frustrating and exhausting to have to process the many decisions we have to make, and then we worry about if we made the right decision, because our knowledge and insight are limited, and not knowing if we made the right decision can cause anxiety. Oh, but how wonderful it is to know that we serve a God who will never leave us to figure things out for ourselves. If you are spending time at the Master's feet, trust that the Holy Spirit within you will instruct and teach you. The Holy Spirit will lead you into all Truth and Righteousness; you just have to ask Him and be receptive to His leading! If you desire good and sound instructions, allow the Holy Spirit to teach you the ways of the Lord. It is always God's desire to lead us with love and wisdom. Because I trust His infinite knowledge and He knows what is best for me, I choose to follow His lead. What about you?

Prayer:

Father, today I surrender my ways, thoughts, ideas, and will unto You. You know the best path for me. Your ways and Your thoughts are pure and perfect. I know that You are gentle and will never force Yourself upon me. Therefore, I am asking You to guide me with Your eyes. Forgive me for the times that I was stubborn and went my own way. Holy Spirit, instruct and teach me the ways of the Father. In Jesus's majestic name, Amen!

Your prayer for today:

____

____

____

____

____

Notes:

DAY NINE

Isaiah 26:4: "Trust ye in the Lord, forever, for in the Lord Jehovah is everlasting strength."

Life Application:

There is so much going on in the world. The demands of family, marriages, education, ministry, or whatever you may be facing, can sometimes seem massive and if we are not careful, we will find ourselves drowning in life's demands. We are human and our strength is limited. Our frame is fragile, and we are not designed to carry inordinate demands or cares. Jesus offers to lighten the load for us, and He tells us to cast our cares upon Him. We hear Him, but so often, we neglect His Word and we continue to struggle and carry the load of life all by ourselves! Today, if you are feeling weak, faint, and do not feel as though you can take another step, STOP where you are and remind yourself that your strength is in Jehovah God! When you are weak, that is when He can reveal His strength and might on your behalf! Wow, that reminder just took a load off of me. The beauty in serving the all-powerful mighty God is that He never gets tired, weary, sleepy, or faint. We have access to His strength twenty-four seven, whenever we need it. His strength is limitless; He is our everlasting Rock!

Prayer:

Father, You are the Rock of my salvation and strength. Your strength is from everlasting to everlasting. Because of your unlimited strength that dwells within me, I can courageously face this day. Lord, forgive me for the times that I depended upon my own abilities and strength and forgot to call upon You for help. Lord, in Your infinite love, continue to remind me that You care about me and You desire for me to cast all my cares upon You and to leave them with You. In Jesus's name, Amen!

Your prayer for today:

____

____

____

____

____

Notes:

DAY TEN

Job 42:2 (Amp): "I know that you can do all things, and that no thought or purpose of yours can be restrained."

Life Application:

This passage of scripture is short, but potent. This verse reminds us of the sovereignty, power, and greatness of our God. It places everything in its proper perspective: that God is always in control and nothing can stop His purpose and/or plan from being fulfilled in your life. When things appear to be out of control in my life or in our society, I meditate on this scripture. What may look like confusion or chaos to me, God has everything under control and nothing can derail or stop His perfect purpose from being fulfilled in my life, your life, and the world. I intentionally reiterate the comfort in knowing that our great Jehovah God can do all things. Nothing is impossible for Him! Let's remember in our chaotic situations, whether they are personal or global, our God will use His divine rearrangement and bring about divine order, and God will always have His way and His way is always Good, acceptable, and perfect! Let's rejoice in that!

Prayer:

Lord, You are Sovereign, mighty, and powerful. Regardless of what my eyes may see or my ears my hear, I am confident that

You have everything under Your Control. Your Word repeatedly speaks to me and encourages me that You can do all things, nothing is impossible for You, and nothing can stop Your purpose from being fulfilled. Chaos and confusion are opportunities for You to reveal Your greatness and Sovereignty. Today, I rest and surrender to Your plan so Your purpose may be established in me. Let Your purpose be done unto me according to your will! In Jesus's name, Amen.

Your prayer for today:

____

____

____

____

____

Notes:

DAY ELEVEN

Job 42:5: "I had heard of you only by the hearing of the ear, but now my (spiritual) eyes see you."

Life Application:

Oh my, how true this is for so many of us. How many of us only have secondhand knowledge of our God? How many of us only know of God through our parents, friends, family members, or only on Sunday morning! Or hearing about Him through the testimonies of others, reading books (perhaps, this book), magazines, devotionals, etc. All of these are good and should be used to increase, confirm, and deepen your relationship with our Lord. They all have their proper place in our spiritual growth, but they should never replace intimate time with the Lord and in His Word. We need one-on-one time with Jesus. We need to have a personal experience, a personal encounter with our Lord and Savior Jesus Christ. It is good at times for us to have a Damascus experience (such as Paul) so our spiritual eyes can be opened. There are so many distractions and hindrances in the world around us that can, at times, dull or even blind us to the things of God. When you feel yourself losing your passion, zeal, and enthusiasm for God and the things of God, it may be that time to ask God to remove the scales off our eyes, so we can see Jesus for who He is as Job did! Could it be your time for a Damascus experience?

Prayer:

Lord, open my spiritual eyes so I can see You high and lifted up. I need to see You lifted above every situation, every circumstance that I am faced with. Lord, remove anything that's blocking my vision, anything on my blindside that's causing a distorted view of You. I desire to experience You on a firsthand, personal level. I'm tired of piggybacking on what everyone else is saying about You; I want my own encounter with Your greatness! I desire to see You as John saw You in Your power, greatness, brilliance, splendor, and glory that caused him to fall as if he was dead! In Jesus's name, Amen!

Your prayer for today:

____

____

____

____

____

Notes:

DAY TWELVE

Isaiah 49:16: "Behold, I have graven thee upon the palms of my hand; thy walls are continually before me."

Life Application:

There may be times that it may appear that God is so far away. Even though His Word confirms that, He will never leave us. We sometimes feel alone, in a dark place, deserted from His presence. Friend, rest assured, God is faithful to His Word. When we begin to feel that God has left us, first, let's check our proximity to God. In other words, have we deserted Him? Has our busyness gotten in the way of our worship? Have we become distracted by the cares of life, or are we harboring unforgiveness or any unconfessed sin? After we have examined and ridden ourselves of distractions, obstacles, hindrances, etc., then we can comfort ourselves in knowing that God has never left us and He is always intentionally and deliberately thinking about us. This scripture strongly lets us (metaphorically) know that we are always on God's mind; He tells us that He has graven us out upon His palms. Every time He opens His hands and looks down, He sees your face, and He sees my face! Think about your face in the palm of God's hand the next time you feel the Lord has left you. He will not leave us, because we are forever imprinted in His hands.

Prayer:

Father, at times it appears that You are so far from me. I feel as though I have nowhere to turn. However, I reflect on Your Word, that I am engraved on the palm of Your hand and this is what gives me the strength to continue to press forward. Father, thank you for always keeping my face before You. In Jesus's name, Amen.

Your prayer for today:

____

____

____

____

____

Notes:

DAY THIRTEEN

Psalm 138:7: "Though I walk in the midst of trouble, thou wilt revive me: thou shalt stretch forth your hand against the wrath of mine enemies, and thy right hand shall save me."

Life Application:

Life situations can sometimes feel overwhelming. The pressure can sometimes feel as though it is taking the very life out of us, leaving us feeling helpless and hopeless. These are the times we need to run to Jesus and not from Him. Only Jesus has the power to revive, restore, strengthen, and totally heal us. We are going to have troubles and afflictions, but the beauty is to know that we are not alone; our Lord sits on the right hand of the Father to save us. Remember, God's right hand of power is where Jesus sits and He will lift us up when we reach out for Him! Grab hold of Jesus's saving hand today.

Prayer:

Father, at times I feel so alone, as though life situations are closing in on me. It appears like the problems are about to overtake me, but Your Word declares that in the midst of my trouble, You will revive me. Lord, I look unto the hills from where my help may come. Lord, I speak restoration, revitalization, and resurrection into my life and circumstances today. Thank you, Lord, for delivering me with Your right hand of strength and power! In Jesus's name, Amen!

Your prayer for today:

____

____

____

____

____

Notes:

DAY FOURTEEN

Numbers 11:23: "And the Lord said unto Moses: Is the Lord's hand waxed short? Thou shall see now whether my Word shall come to pass unto thee or not."

Life Application:

Have you ever been in a position where you know God has promised you something? You wait, you wait, you wait for weeks, then months that turn into years. Then you begin to review your situation, look at your limited resources, and try to figure out how God is going to accomplish what He promised! In the natural, in our finite mind and thinking, it doesn't seem like God will be able to fulfill His promise. Then we rationalize: surely, we must assist God, because the promise is a big one and God will need our help! Well, friend, let me tell you, God doesn't need our help. He is the Almighty and every promise He made and is still making, He alone is able to bring it to pass without our assistance. Many times our interference can and/or will delay the promise. God's resources are limitless, so if He made you a promise, trust He is able and capable to bring it to pass as He told Moses! With a stretched out arm, He created Heaven and Heaven is unmeasurable. Does this give you an image of the length of His arm?

Prayer:

Father, thank you for being the great infinite God that You are! Your outstretched arms created Heaven; therefore, that confirms Your arms aren't short. Because Your resources are vast, limitless, and endless, I'm placing my complete trust in You to fulfill every promise You made to me in Your perfect timing. In Jesus's name ... Amen.

Your prayer for today:

____

____

____

____

____

Notes:

DAY FIFTEEN

Luke 10:19: "Behold I give unto you power to tread on serpents and scorpions and over all the power of the enemy and nothing by any means shall hurt you."

Life Application:

When we are in that dark hour and it appears that every force of darkness is coming at and against us, we must remember Jesus has given us all power and authority over the enemy. Our enemies are not subject to only people. Our enemy is anything out of the alignment of God's Word and purpose for our lives. Whatever may be causing stress or robbing us of peace, joy, and contentment in Christ is our enemy. We have the power to take control over the situation, bring it into obedience, and submission to Jesus's Lordship! We do not have to allow unpleasant situations and circumstances rule and reign in our lives. I'm not suggesting that we will not experience afflictions, but they will not **rule us!** As long as we are submitted under Christ's Lordship, we have a legal right to command our enemies to align with God's Word! Jesus is the Word and the Word said, "Nothing by any means shall hurt you." Do you believe the Word, aka Jesus?

Prayer:

Lord, I take authority over every situation, every circumstance (you can be specific) that has come up against me and my family. You said that You have given me all power and authority over the enemy, and I'm treading upon this situation and it shall not overtake, rule, reign, control, or hurt me according to your Word. In Jesus's name, Amen.

Your prayer for today:

____

____

____

____

____

Notes:

DAY SIXTEEN

2 Timothy 1:7: "For God has not given us the Spirit of fear, but of power, love and of a sound mind."

Life Application:

It is human nature to be afraid of the unknown. Venturing out on any new life circumstance, such as a job, college, retirement, marriage, starting a family, starting life alone due to loss of loved one, or divorce can create anxiety within us. Anticipation of tomorrow can create anxiety because no one but God knows the future. God is omniscient (all-knowing). As believers, we can rest in God's all-knowing ability. He is in our "today" and seen in our "tomorrow"! Although, we may not know what tomorrow holds, God does and if He is in control of our lives, our tomorrow will be perfect, because we serve a perfect God that operates on His perfect timing! Therefore, we can live fearlessly, releasing power, love, and wisdom throughout our days and into the lives of others.

Prayer:

Lord, this day I choose to walk in power, love, and wisdom. It is because of Your grace and love that gives me the confidence to confront every situation with supernatural strength and courage.

I can have a sound mind and make rational decisions, because Your Holy Spirit lives within me and your wisdom and power are infinite. In Jesus's name, Amen.

Your prayer for today:

____

____

____

____

____

Notes:

DAY SEVENTEEN

Acts 4:29-30: "Lord … grant unto thy servants that with all boldness they may speak thou Word (30) by stretching forth thine hand to heal, and that signs and wonders may be done by the name of thy Holy Child, Jesus."

Life Application:

We were created and we were saved to bring honor and glory to Jesus. We are to be a witness unto Jesus and we cannot do this in our own power and strength. We need to be empowered by the Holy Spirit. Yes, we need to be full of His Spirit to tell others about His goodness, love, and plan of salvation. Have you ever tried to minister to someone or tell them about Jesus and the words didn't flow? It seemed really awkward! We aren't effective ministers of the Gospel in our flesh. We have to rely on the power of the Holy Spirit for everything! It is He that works in us to fulfill God's purpose. Jesus told His disciples they would receive power after the Holy Spirit came upon them and they shall be witnesses unto Him. If you are struggling in this area, pray that God will grace you with the needed boldness to be an effective witness unto Him.

Prayer:

Lord, grant me the boldness and confidence to proclaim Your Gospel wherever I go! Download Your words, thoughts, and ideas into my mind so that they will flow out of my mouth and grasp the heart of the hearer and create a hunger and thirst after You. Confirm Your Word with signs and wonders that all mankind will know that You are the One and Only True God. In Jesus's name, Amen.

Your prayer for today:

____

____

____

____

____

Notes:

DAY EIGHTEEN

Matthew 7:7: "Ask and keep on asking and it will be given to you; seek and keep on seeking and you will find; knock and keep on knocking and the door will be opened to you."

Life Application:

This scripture encourages us and confirms that it is God's desire for us to ask for His blessings. He wants us to be persistent in seeking Him for His good gifts. Our God is a good and generous God and wants to bestow His goodness upon those that diligently seek Him. He also wants us to be an active participant, and our involvement is demonstrated in our asking, seeking, and knocking. God knows what is best for us and He will only give us His best. Remember, all good and perfect gifts come from Him. God's storehouse is plentiful; it will never run dry and we never have to worry about bankrupting Heaven. The gifts are endless. We gain access to God's treasure through prayer, studying the scriptures, and spending intimate quiet time in His presence. Ask your Heavenly Father to bless you beyond measure!

Prayer:

Father, thank you for all Your promises. Your word tells me to ask, seek, and knock and I shall receive the good gifts You have in store for me. I am asking You and intentionally seeking You to (name situation). You are a generous God that takes pleasure in giving good gifts to Your children. Thank you for opening the door for me to passionately pursue You. In Jesus's name, Amen!

Your prayer for today:

____

____

____

____

____

Notes:

DAY NINETEEN

1 Corinthians 2:9: "But as it is written, eye hath not seen, nor ear heard, neither have entered into the heart of man, the things which God hath prepared for them that love Him."

Life Application:

Do you love the Lord? If you answered "yes," your spirit should start leaping for joy! I'm not speaking of lip service, but a genuine heartfelt love where your total being is wrapped up in Jesus. If this is you, be encouraged that no matter what you are facing today, trust that God has something great in store for you beyond your wildest imaginations. God has not stopped performing miracles and He is waiting to perform a miracle in your life. The mystery of salvation was hidden for ages and God revealed the mystery to us, which is Christ Jesus! If He gave us Himself, imagine what is available to us through Jesus. So, wipe your tears, throw your shoulders back, lift your head, and shout with the voice of victory!

Prayer:

Father, no matter what I may see and or hear, I will place my trust in You and Your Word. Although things may appear dark, Your Word tells me that eyes haven't seen, nor ears heard, nor have entered into the heart of man, the things that You have prepared for those that love You. Lord, You know the deep intent of my heart. I love You with every part of my being. Therefore, I will wait patiently for You to bestow Your treasure upon me. In Jesus's name, Amen!

Your prayer for today:

____

____

____

____

____

Notes:

DAY TWENTY

Philippians 4:6-7: "Be careful for nothing, but in everything by prayer and supplication with thanksgiving, let your requests be made known unto God. (7) And the Peace of God which passeth all understanding, shall keep your hearts and minds through Christ Jesus."

Life Application:

We are living in unprecedented times of uncertainties. We are living in a society that's rapidly deteriorating and declining! The world we once knew is changing before our very eyes. Confusion and chaos have grabbed our society and everyone is seeking peace in all the wrong places. There is no peace unless you are in Christ and Christ is in you. We were created to find our resting place in God. However, sin has separated humanity from enjoying an intimate relationship with our Creator. But all is not lost, God has made a provision for us and His name is Jesus. Jesus has made it possible where we can come to the Father and let our requests be known. In the midst of all the confusion that surrounds us, Jesus will comfort our hearts with the peace of God. If you have found peace with God, you can enjoy the peace of God.

Prayer:

Father, Your Word tells me not to be anxious, but come to You boldly with my request. Lord, I praise You and give You thanks for everything that You have done for me and for the things that You will do. Father, I confidently bring this request to You, knowing that You hear me and You will respond. My heart and mind are continually on You; therefore, I will rest in Your Peace. In Jesus's name, Amen.

Your prayer for today:

____

____

____

____

____

Notes:

DAY TWENTY-ONE

Psalm 55:22: "Cast thy burden upon the Lord, and He shall sustain thee; He shall never suffer the righteous to be moved."

Life Application:

Wow, what a powerful promise! The Lord wants us to bring Him our cares, our struggles, our anxieties. He wants to carry our load on His broad shoulders. The sins of the entire world were placed upon Him, so surely He can handle our little burden! However, He is not going to take it from us or force us to give it to Him. He wants to see our faith, our trust in willingly surrendering everything to Him. You may be going through something right now. It may seem as though your back is against the wall; you do not see any way out. Take a step back and remind the Lord that He said you can cast your cares upon Him and trust that He will sustain You in times of trouble.

Your shoulders aren't wide or big enough to carry the burden. Give them all to Jesus! Our God is holding the entire universe together by the power of His Word, all one hundred billion galaxies that make up the universe, so surely, He can handle our little problems!

Prayer:

Lord, this situation is too heavy for me to bear (you can name the situation). Just as I trusted You to save me from the power of darkness, I must trust You and relinquish this situation(s) unto You. Your shoulders are broader and You can handle the load. I am casting my burdens at Your feet, and according to Your Word, You will sustain me and not allow me to be moved. In Jesus's name, Amen.

Your prayer for today:

____

____

____

____

____

Notes:

DAY TWENTY-TWO

Jeremiah 30:17: "For I will restore health unto thee and I will heal thee of thy wounds saith the Lord.

Life Application:

Yes, God created doctors. He gave them the wisdom and knowledge to understand the human body. However, let's not forget He is the Great Physician. He is the ultimate Healer. He so wonderfully and intricately designed our bodies, our innermost being. Therefore, He knows how every part of the human body should function. Our God is not only concerned and wants to heal our physical body, He also wants to heal and restore us spiritually, mentally, emotionally, and in every area of our existence. In other words, God wants us to be complete in Him. As we seek God to restore our health, remember God wants to restore the entire man. He desires wholeness for us. As we seek the Lord, for total restoration, remember the most important healing is our spirit!

Prayer:

Lord, You are Jehovah Rapha, my healer, my great physician. I speak and decree, strength, healing, and restoration to my entire being. I demand every part of my being from the crown of my head to the sole of my feet to align with Your Word and function the way You designed and intended. In Jesus's name, Amen.

Your prayer for today:

____

____

____

____

____

Notes:

DAY TWENTY-THREE

1 John 4:4: "Ye are of God, little children, and have overcome them, because greater is He that is in you, than he that is in the world."

Life Application:

In this life we are going to face many trials, tribulations, obstacles, and struggles. Jesus didn't promise us a perfect life or a life void of problems, but He did promise us perfect peace, as we stay in Him. He also, promised, whatever struggles we are confronted with, He is with us. He will always be with us, and we never have to worry about being alone. This promise is fulfilled in the person of the "Holy Spirit" that indwells in every believer. Because He has overcome the world, we can face every challenge with overcoming confidence, because the Overcomer lives within us! The Jesus in us is bigger than anything that we will ever face.

Prayer:

Lord, help me see You for the vast limitless, conquering God that You are. When I see the grandeur of who You are, I see myself as an overcomer. I stand on Your Word today, that this problem (be specific) will not overtake me, because greater is He that is within me than He that controls the air. I take authority over all the powers of darkness that have been released and assigned to me. In Jesus's name, Amen!

Your prayer for today:

____

____

____

____

____

Notes:

DAY TWENTY-FOUR

Matthew 16:19: "And I will give unto thee the keys of the kingdom of heaven and whatsoever thou shalt bind on Earth shall be bound in heaven and whatsoever thou shall loose on Earth, shall be loose in Heaven."

Life Application:

As believers in Christ, God wants us to understand that we are His legal authority on Earth. The authority that was once handed over to Satan has been legally taken away by our Lord and Savior Jesus Christ! This authority has been given back to humanity through the believing and acceptance of Jesus Christ's finished work on Calvary. Jesus has given us the keys to destroy the works of the devil that is running havoc and chaos in our lives, lives of others, and in our world! One of these keys is prayer. Saints, we have to learn how to effectively use this key if we truly want to see the power of God move in history. Prayer is the transformation key! It is the key that brings about changes. Whatever we deem unlawful on earth, God says, He will back us up. It will be deemed unlawful in Heaven. We do not have to accept Satan's unlawful acts and illegal activity in our lives or the lives of others. Heaven is in agreement with us! Keys are to lock and unlock doors, so pray and ask the Holy Spirit to reveal to you how to effectively use your keys and begin to unlock and release some of Heaven's goodness into earth!

Prayer:

Father, thank you for the keys and access to the Kingdom of Heaven. I come against this unlawful situation that has confronted me. I am using my key of prayer and I am binding this situation (name the situation) in Jesus's name and I am releasing (name what you are releasing) into my life and over the circumstance in Jesus's name! Father, let loose from Heaven favor, grace, mercy, and joy (whatever you need at this time bring it down in the spirit). Lord, let your will be done on earth as it is in Heaven! In Jesus's name, Amen.

Your prayer for today:

____

____

____

____

____

Notes:

DAY TWENTY-FIVE

Philippians 4:19: "But my God shall supply all your needs according to His riches and glory in Christ Jesus."

Life Application:

It is easy to become anxious and frustrated when the devil deceives us in thinking that our needs aren't being satisfied. As a believer in Christ, we can be confident that Jesus knows our every need and He has unlimited ways and resources to meet our needs. However, many of us confuse the difference between our needs, wants, and desires. God will fulfill our wants and desires according to His time and within His will. God knows exactly what we need, how much we need, and when it's needed! His Word assures us that He will provide all our needs. This is not a promise of wealth, riches, power, or abundance of material possessions. But we can stand firm on this promise that we will never lack in our basic needs being fulfilled as long as Christ is our Provider, our Source for everything!

Prayer:

Jehovah Jireh, You are my provider! You are my Source! Your ways, resources, and methods are unlimited. There is no end to Your supply source. Therefore, I am trusting You to meet this need (be specific of need) from the rich endless treasures in Christ! In Jesus's majestic name, Amen.

Your prayer for today:

____

____

____

____

____

Notes:

DAY TWENTY-SIX

2 Corinthians 5:17: "Therefore if any man be in Christ, he is a new creature, old things are passed away, behold all things become new."

Life Application:

Wow, this is good news! Once we accept Christ as our Lord and Savior, He gives us a brand new life in Him. A life of hope, abundance, and security. Our new Christian Life is not a life of reformation, rehabilitation, or reeducation, but it is a life of transformation. We are actually new creatures, new beings! God has given us the opportunity to begin a new life, with a new Master. Your past life doesn't determine your future in Christ. Our old "self" was crucified with Christ and we rose in the newness of life with Him. I encourage you to walk boldly and confidently in your new life with Christ. Do not allow anyone to shame or condemn you for who you used to be!

Prayer:

Father, I thank you for sending Your only begotten Son to die for me. Because of Jesus's obedience to death and my acceptance of His completed work at Calvary, I am alive by His indwelling Holy Spirit. Lord, thank you for a new life, a life of freedom, abundance, joy, and peace in Christ. Because I am a new creature in Christ, I shall walk in the newness of life. In Jesus's glorious name, Amen!

Your prayer for today:

Notes:

DAY TWENTY-SEVEN

Romans 8:28: "And we know that all things work together for good to them that love God, to them who are called according to His purpose."

Life Application:

Believers, if this is the only scripture you have in your spiritual arsenal, it will get you through every struggle, challenge, and/or trial. This scripture reflects God's Sovereignty and Providence. He speaks of His unlimited power and untouchable authority. We live in a world where evil is prevalent, and because of the sovereignty and prowess of our God, He has the ability to turn every situation around for our good. This scripture points me to the life of Joseph (**Genesis 37-50**). In summation, Joseph went from the pit to prison to the palace, all by the divine orchestrating of God's Sovereign and providential power! What was meant for his harm, God turned it around for his good. However, there is a caveat in this scripture. Do not ignore the last segment of the scripture: "for them that love God to them who are called according to His purpose." Yes, God will work everything out for those that love Him and fulfill His purpose. Believers, we must always remember that it is always about God's honor and glory. If we trust in God and look to Heaven for our security, we can stand boldly on this truth and watch God work out our situation.

Prayer:

Father, I may not like what I am facing today, but I can accept the pain, hurt, and disappointment because my trust is in You. I know that I love You and I am called according to Your purpose. I am fulfilling this purpose to the best of my knowledge and understanding. Therefore, I am confident that You have worked everything out for my good. It may not look good to me, but I know that it is good for me, because my life is in Your hands. In Jesus's name, Amen.

Your prayer for today:

____

____

____

____

____

Notes:

DAY TWENTY-EIGHT

2 Thessalonians 3:3: "But the Lord is faithful, who shall establish you, and keep you from evil."

Life Application:

We can always depend upon the faithfulness of God. God is a promise and covenant keeper. We live in a society that is rapidly declining and deteriorating, with humanity turning away from God. New ways of being wicked and evil are discovered daily. But the Lord is always in control. Even in the midst of confusion, calamity, and chaos, God can and will continue to establish, strengthen, and perfect His work in His faithful saints. Not only can He sustain us, He knows how to keep evil from overtaking us. God is not moved by the external circumstances going on in the world. The devastations don't catch Him off guard. He is not at a loss when He sees storms, earthquakes, wars, plagues, pestilences, or any other calamity. It may appear out of control to us, but know that everything is in God's control. Allow God to establish you and keep you securely in His loving arms away from evil!

Prayer:

Father, You have proven your faithfulness to me numerous times. Regardless of what things may look like, I know that You are able to sustain and keep Your children safe. I trust the good work that You began in me, You will bring to fruition. You will establish me, protect me, and keep me from this present evil. In Jesus's name, Amen!

Your prayer for today:

____

____

____

____

____

Notes:

DAY TWENTY-NINE

John 11:25: "Jesus said unto her, I am the Resurrection and the Life; he that believes in Me, though he were dead, yet shall he live."

Life Application:

Because He lives forevermore, we can live. Jesus's resurrection is proof that He conquered death and that He is the Son of God with all power and dominion. We all were once dead in our trespasses, being alienated from God, enemies of the Lord. Because of Jesus's obedience to the cross, God raised Him from the dead and all mankind have the opportunity to believe and enjoy everlasting life with God! Without Jesus, we have no life. He is our lifeline. Until we accept Jesus as our Lord and Savior, we are the walking dead! He has the power over life and death and the power to forgive us of all our sins. It is amazing that Jesus spoke of His resurrection before His death! This is evidence that He was God in the flesh. Trust Jesus who is Life to restore your life and resurrect your dead situations/ circumstances. Only God will have this kind of insight and foresight into the future. We see the omniscient nature of our God in the person of Jesus.

Prayer:

Jesus, I believe that You are the Resurrection and the Life. You are the only begotten Son of God. Lord, because You have the power over life and death, I place the life that You gave me in your hands. I am confident that You can resurrect every dead area in my life, so that I can be a fruit-producing witness unto You. In Jesus's name, Amen.

Your prayer for today:

____

____

____

____

____

Notes:

DAY THIRTY

Jeremiah 1:18: "Now, behold I have made thee this day a defenced City, and an iron pillar, and bronzen walls against the land, against the kings of Judah, against the princes thereof and against the people of the land."

Life Application:

Are there times when you may feel weak and outnumbered by your enemies? Have you ever looked at your enemies and/or circumstances and thought that there wasn't any way you would overcome what was before you? I have been there! This scripture reminds us that God has strengthened us to face every battle. It is not by coincidence that He uses this military word to describe our position. God has made us strong; He has strengthened and secured us to be victorious in this life. A fortified city has high stone, wood, or brick walls to protect it from invaders. An iron pillar symbolizes one who is strong, unyielding, and immovable. Let this comfort your spirit. Because He dwells within us, we are as the high brick wall that is secure from invaders!

Prayer:

Thank you, Lord, for making me a fortified city, an iron pillar, and as bronze walls against all my enemies. Although my enemies outnumber me, they shall not prevail against me, for You have established me to be unyielding and immovable. In Jesus's majesty name, Amen.

Your prayer for today:

____

____

____

____

____

Notes:

DAY THIRTY-ONE

Ephesians 1:3: "Blessed be the God and Father of our Lord Jesus Christ, who hath blessed us with all spiritual blessings in heavenly places in Christ."

Life Application:

Wow! God has already given us everything we need to live a victorious life. Jesus completed His assignment so we can enjoy a blessed life on Earth as well as throughout eternity with Father God ! So, you may be saying, "Why aren't I experiencing this blessed, victorious life in history (on Earth)? Well, that's because our blessings are in heavenly places (the spiritual realm) and we have to learn how to position ourselves to pull them down into history (Earth). In other words, we have to learn how to live from Heaven to Earth, with a heavenly perspective on everything, speaking Heaven's language. That's why it's imperative that we learn and pray the Word of God. God wants us to operate from a spiritual perspective to release the spiritual blessings that are stored in the heavenly. As you pray this scripture, ask God to help you position yourself to operate from a heavenly perspective so you can begin to live and experience your blessed, victorious life on Earth.

Prayer:

Lord, thank you for blessing me with everything I need to enjoy a blessed and victorious life on Earth. It is because of Jesus's completed work at the cross and His seat at Your right hand that I have access to all Heaven's benefits. There is no lack or deficiency in my life because Your word assures me that You have already blessed me with all spiritual blessings in Christ. Father, show me how to operate from my spiritual position in Christ and release all You have for me. In Jesus's glorious name, Amen.

Your prayer for today:

____

____

____

____

____

Notes:

DAY THIRTY-TWO

John 14:13: "And whatsoever, ye shall ask in my name, that I will do, that the Father may be glorified in the Son."

Life Application:

To put this in its proper context and understanding, God will grant us our prayers when they align with His will. God knows what is best for us and He will not give us anything that he knows will hurt us, harm us, and pull us away from Him. In the ancient Hebrew tradition, "prayer" meant calling on the name of the Lord, which equated to immersing oneself in God's presence. That's what we are doing when we pray; we are immersing ourselves in the presence of the Lord as if He is right in front of us, surrounding us with His presence. We must be in grace and in right standing with Him to be immersed in His presence. We are reminded in scripture that no flesh (sin) shall glory in His presence. Jesus continues to let us know that we must continually keep His Words and continually abide in Him. As we continue to abide in Jesus, we are aligning our will and desires with the Father. We are allowing Him to imprint His desires and His will for us upon our hearts. Then we can boldly approach the Throne and ask in Jesus's name, and whatever we ask according to His will the Father will grant it and therefore the Father will be glorified. Remember, everything that God does for us is to bring honor and glory to Him. We will benefit, but it is always about His name! Knowing this, go and immerse yourself in the presence of God and ask whatsoever in the name of Jesus!

Prayer:

Father, I come to You in the name of Jesus, the name that is above all names. I ask you in Jesus's name, to (cite your need, your petitions). Lord, You said whatsoever I ask in Your name, You will honor; and I know that I am asking according to Your will, because this will advance Your Kingdom on Earth and bring honor and glory to You. Lord, I thank you for answering this prayer in Jesus's name, Amen!

Your prayer for today:

____

____

____

____

____

Notes:

DEVELOP YOUR PRAYER FROM THE FOLLOWING SCRIPTURES

Think about what you are facing today and incorporate the following scriptures in your prayer.

Let's begin putting our voice to these selected scriptures and develop a prayer around them!

Job 22:28: "Thou shalt also decree a thing, and it shall be established unto thee, and the light shall shine upon thy ways."

Your Prayer:

____

____

____

____

____

Isaiah 26:3: "Thou will keep him in perfect peace, whose mind is stayed on thee."

Your Prayer:

____

____

____

____

____

1 Timothy 2:1-2: "I exhort therefore, that, first of all, supplications, prayers, intercessions and giving of thanks, be made for all men; (2) for kings, and for all that are in authority; that we may lead a quiet and peaceable life in all godliness and honesty."

Your Prayer:

____

____

____

____

____

Numbers 23:19: "God is not a man, that he should lie, neither the son of man that he should repent. Hath he said, and shall he not do it? Or hath he spoken and shall he not make it good?"

Your Prayer:

____

____

____

____

____

Jeremiah 29:11: "For I know the thoughts that I think toward you, saith the Lord, thoughts of peace and not of evil, to give you an expected end."

Your Prayer:

____

____

____

____

____

Proverbs 22:6: "Train up a child in the way he should go; and when he is old, he will not depart from it."

Your Prayer:

____

____

____

____

____

Deuteronomy 31:6: "Be strong and of a good courage, fear not, nor be afraid of them: for the LORD thy God, he it is that doth go with thee; he will not fail thee, nor forsake thee."

Your Prayer:

____

____

____

____

____

Psalm 23:2: “He maketh me to lie down in green pastures: He leadeth me beside the still waters.”

Your Prayer:

Job 12:13: “With him is wisdom and strength, He hath counsel and understanding.”

Your Prayer:

Hopefully, you are becoming a pro at praying God's Word. By praying God's Word, your prayers are intentional, deliberate, and hitting your target! You are going to be amazed as you see Heaven open up and our Father of Glory begin to release the answers to your prayers. Now, let's move to specific prayers for everyday situations!

TARGETED SCRIPTURES FOR SPECIFIC NEEDS

These next set of scriptures we can pray over our lives, into our lives, and in situations whenever we are confronted with specific challenges. God has the answer for everything that we will ever need in life. The prescription for all our aliments is in God's Word, the Holy Scriptures. I have categorized them into the most common areas we all have faced, or will face at some point, in our lives. Remember, our goal is to hit our target and cripple the powers of darkness trying to handicap, cripple, or prevent us from fulfilling our purpose in Christ.

As you pray these scriptures into your life, family, surroundings, and circumstances, please continue to develop your unique prayer using the Word!

Scriptures for Your Children

When you are praying over and into your child's life, you are asking God to perform His Word in their lives.

Isaiah 54:13: "And all thy children shall be taught of the LORD; and great shall be the peace of thy children."

Colossians 3:20: "Children obey your parents in all things: for this is well pleasing unto the Lord."

Luke 2:52: "And Jesus increased in wisdom and stature and in favor with God and man (replace Jesus with your child's name)." You are praying that God will increase your child with favor.

Psalm 115:14: "The LORD shall increase you more and more, You and your children."

Scriptures for Healing Physical, Mental, Emotional Problems or Whatever You Need Healing

Jeremiah 17:14: "Heal me, oh Lord, and I shall be healed; save me, and I shall be saved for thou art my praise."

Exodus 23:25: "And ye shall serve the Lord God and He shall bless thy bread and thy water, and I will take sickness away from the midst of thee."

1 Peter 2:24: "Who His own self bare our sins in His own body on the tree, that we, being dead to sins, should live unto righteousness: by whose stripes ye were healed."

3 John 1:2: "Beloved, I wish above all things, that thou mayest prosper and be in health, even as thy soul prospereth."

Scriptures for Godly Wisdom

Psalm 111:10: "The fear of the LORD is the beginning of wisdom: a good understanding have all that do His commandments; His praise endureth forever."

Proverbs 2:6: "For the LORD giveth wisdom: out of his mouth cometh knowledge and understanding."

James 1:5: "If any of you lack wisdom, let him ask of God, that giveth to all men liberally, and upbraideth not; and it shall be given him."

Psalm 90:12: "So teach us to number our days, that we may apply our hearts unto wisdom."

Scriptures for God's Protection

There are so many scriptures we can pray over our lives for God's firewall of protection. Here are a few you may want to include in your arsenal.

Ephesians 6:11: "Put on the whole armor of God, that you may be able to stand against the wiles of the devil."

Psalm 32:7: "Thou art my hiding place; thou shalt preserve me from trouble; thou shalt compass me about with songs of deliverance."

Deuteronomy 31:3: "The LORD thy God, he will go over before thee, and He will destroy these nations from before thee, and thou shalt possess them …"

Psalm 91:2: "I will say of the LORD, He is my refuge and my fortress: my God; in Him will I trust."

Scriptures for Peace

John 16:33: "These things I have spoken unto you, that in me ye might have peace. In the world ye shall have tribulation; but be of good cheer, I have overcome the world."

John 14:27: "Peace I leave with you, my peace I give you, not as the world giveth, give I unto you. Let not your heart be troubled, neither let it be afraid."

2 Thessalonians 3:16: "Now the Lord of peace, himself give you peace always by all means."

Numbers 24-26: "The Lord bless thee, and keep thee; (v25) The Lord make his face shine upon thee, and be gracious unto thee; (v26) The Lord lift up His countenance upon thee, and give thee peace."

Scriptures on Strength

Psalm 121:1-2: "I will lift up mine eyes unto the hills, from whence cometh my help; (v2) My help cometh from the Lord, which made heaven and earth."

Exodus 15:2: "The Lord is my strength and song, and he is become my salvation: He is my God, and I will prepare Him a habitation; My father's God and I will exalt Him."

Joshua 1:9: "Have not I commanded thee? Be strong and of good courage; be not afraid, neither be thou dismayed: for the LORD thy God is with thee whithersoever thou goest."

1 Peter 5:10: "But the God of all grace, who hath called us unto his eternal glory by Christ Jesus, after that ye have suffered a while, make you perfect, stablish, strengthen, settle you."

This is not intended to be an exhaustive list of scriptures for every specific need. The goal is to provide a framework and assist you in establishing and strengthening your connection with God through praying His Word. Be creative, get your journal out, and develop your own scripture list for your specific needs. Make your intimate time with God fun and purposeful.

CONCLUSION

The purpose of this devotional book is not to view God as a genie, Santa Claus, or magician, but to see Him as the great I Am that has called us to partner with Him to advance His Kingdom on Earth.

I pray that this compilation of scriptures and prayers has encouraged you to purposefully and intentionally begin to study and memorize scriptures. I pray that you do not stop with these thirty-two scriptures and prayers, but you allow the Holy Spirit to increase your knowledge and understanding of Him and His Word. I pray that every person that reads this book is inspired by the Holy Spirit to put their voice to God's Word and watch Him come for His Word!

As you begin to incorporate the scriptures into your prayers, you will begin to see and experience an explosive transformation in your life, surroundings, and environment, wherever you go. The Word of God is Spirit and Life and it creates and brings life wherever it is spoken. **John 1:1** states: "In the beginning was the Word and the Word was with God and the Word was God." God is the only person that can create and give life, and Jesus Christ is God in the flesh. In short, you need Jesus to quicken whatever is dead in your life, even if that is you! Reflect on the truth, that God created the entire universe with His Word, the universe held together by the power of His Word! Can we dare to believe that He can uphold us together by the power of His

Word? He has delegated that power and authority to you and me.

Beloved, the devil is not afraid of "our" words. The only person he is afraid of and cannot defeat is Jesus, the Word of God, who is God. When you pray the scriptures, you are releasing Jesus's authority and power, and Satan cannot withstand the power of God. He has to surrender and obey the Word of God. Put your voice to God's Word and decapitate, stifle, and cripple the enemy's power over you.

Pray the Word of God over your life, marriage, children, friends, job, ministry, school, city, state, nation, coworkers, church—everything you can think of!

Boldly approach God's throne and talk to Him about what you know He loves to hear, His Word!

I pray God's peace and blessing upon every reader of this book!

HAVE A BLESSED LIFE!

PRAYER OF REPENTANCE AND SALVATION

Acceptance of the Father's Free Gift of Love, Jesus Christ!

You are saved by faith in Jesus Christ! Everyone who calls upon the name of the Lord shall be saved (**Romans 10:13**). If you desire to come into the Family of God and become a joint heir with Jesus, confess with your mouth and believe in your heart the following prayer:

> Father, I come to you through your Son, Jesus Christ, who died for my sins. I acknowledge that I am a sinner, and need to repent to be forgiven of my sins. I must acknowledge and believe in my heart and confess with my mouth that Jesus shed His blood and died on the cross. You raised Him on the third day, so I may be cleansed and forgiven of all sin—past, present, and future—and can enjoy eternal life with You! Lord Jesus, I ask you to forgive me of all sin. I surrender my life to You as my Lord and Savior. From this day forward, I am now a child of God and a citizen of Your Heavenly Kingdom. In Jesus's glorious name, Amen.

You have now accepted the Father's free gift of Love, which is Jesus Christ! Welcome to the Family of Faith. If you desire more information about salvation, forgiveness, and repentance, I encourage you to read the following scriptures: **Romans 9:10**, **Romans 3:23**, **Matthew 19:25-26**, and **Philippians 3:4-11**. These are just a few scriptures to assist you with understanding your new faith. I also encourage you to connect to like-minded believers and ask the Holy Spirit to lead you to a Faith-Word teaching church.

Keep your eyes on Jesus and continue to grow in the Faith! God bless you!

OTHER BOOKS AND READINGS BY THIS AUTHOR:

Lord, I Shall Be a House of Prayer! Developing a Relationship with Jesus by Toni Allen

You may also visit www.sbprabooks.com/ToniAllen for short inspirational blogs.

REVIEW REQUESTED:

We'd like to know if you enjoyed the book.
Please consider leaving a review on the platform
from which you purchased the book.

CPSIA information can be obtained
at www.ICGtesting.com
Printed in the USA
LVHW111227230223
740172LV00005B/251

9 781682 357552